Table of Contents

Editor: NM Gerald A. Larson, PhD

ISBN 978-1-7361539-0-1
Library of Congress Catalog Number 2021900511

Preface

I am a level IV US Chess Federation National Chess Coach. My proven method displayed herein is ground breaking for beginner chess players and teachers of the game of chess.

Chess is not an easy game to play really well or to learn for that matter. Until now! There is a great degree of understanding and knowledge about the game one must acquire to be considered playing well. Playing well is a relative statement when it comes to playing chess. To me (playing well) means you play with understanding and a high degree of well-established chess principles to guide your play. Thus, allowing you to win and enjoy the chess experience! This process of learning to play chess well could take most people years. Most learn through trial and era. I have found most chess beginner books have overlooked several important elements when it comes to games people play, especially children. They have overlooked the fun aspect. If a game is not fun to learn (Chess) many won't bother getting to the rich and beautiful experience that chess really is. Understanding is another overlooked aspect that has been missing in beginners' books leaving the student confused. A new way to teach chess had to be invented for the new mind of the planet. They think at a faster rate. Reward must come quickly for the new generation. They want it now. I am here to teach the game of chess just the way they want it fast, using understanding to teach. I have taught many state champions. Three of my students have been the best in the country on their level. Many in the top twenty, and one has gone on to become the World Cadets Champion for girls under 12. All of my students started with this system of learning. And they improved at lightning speed. Seeing their success inspired me to share this method with students and teachers helping to spread chess to all who wish to play, however have been frustrated trying to learn or teach chess. Teaching endgames first is the way of old. The method in this book is for this new generation of humans. Going from this is how a pawn moves to checkmate is a long journey if done the old way. I have reinvented the wheel of learning chess for beginners. This book will change everything. Let's begin.

1   The Board, the Men, and Chess Notation

Because this is a book, the reader will first need to understand some chess terms and how chess positions and chess game scores are written down.

Here is the board. It consist of 64 squares. 32 light squares and 32 dark squares.

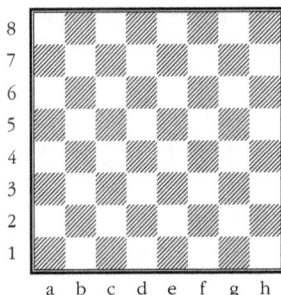

The vertical lines on the board are called **files**, and they are named by letters a through h.

The horizontal lines on the board are called **ranks**, and they are named by numbers 1 through 8.

Each **square** is the intersection of a file and a rank, and is named accordingly. For example, the lower-right corner square is named h1.

The other (skewed) lines on the board are **diagonals**, and they are named with their endpoint squares. All the squares in a diagonal are the same color. For example, the longest light-squared diagonal is a8-h1 (or h1-a8).

The men are:

♟	the **pawn**
♞	the **knight**, written N
♝	the **bishop**, written B
♜	the **rook**, written R
♛	the **queen**, written Q
♚	the **king**, written K

There are two kinds of men: pawns and **pieces**. A knight or bishop is a **minor piece**; a rook, queen, or king is a **major piece**.

The action in a game is written move by move, specifying what man moved and where. For example, **3.Nf3** means white's third move was a knight to the f3 square, and **5...Bc6** means Black's fifth move was a bishop to the c6 square. The "pawn" part is not written down to record a pawn move, so **1.e4** is moving the e-file pawn to e4.

There are a few common special language-invariant notations: "+" is check, "#" is checkmate, and "?" indicates a bad move.

2 The Pawn Game

The pawn game is a method to allow people of all ages to quickly play a variant of chess. This allows them to understand the movement of all the men on the chess board in a fun new way. After all, in order to like any game, you have to be able to win! The pawn game is not new. What is different is my new method and the rules or principles I have added to this game. These rules must be followed to instill discipline in the student. Let's begin by setting up the board that looks like this diagram.

There are two armies: White and Black. White always moves first.

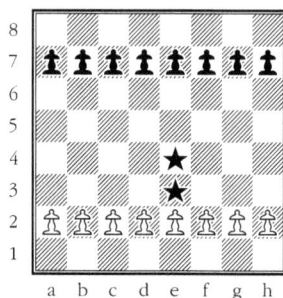

2.1 Meeting

A pawn can move straight forward one or two squares from its original position. After a pawn has moved from its original position, for the rest of the game it can only move one square at a time. It must move straight forward unless it is capturing. The pawn has a value of 1. The pawns can never move backwards. If White moves his e-file pawn 2 squares, and then Black does the same, written **1.e4 e5**, this is called **meeting**, shown below.

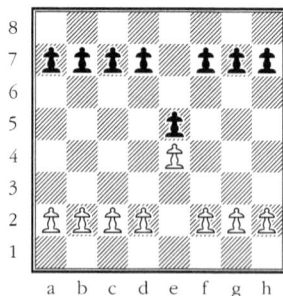

This is the Open Game and will always be the starting position of every game in this book. When pawns **meet** neither can move forward; they block each other's forward movement.

2.2 Touching

The only way the blocked pawn can move is if another pawn moves up into a position where it can be captured. Capturing in chess is different than capturing in checkers. In chess you capture by moving your man onto the square and removing and replacing the man you are capturing. Pawns can only capture (or "take") diagonally forward one square. This situation after **1.d4 e5** is called **touching**. The pawns on squares d4 and e5 are touching each other.

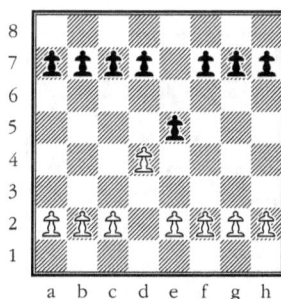

This is my first principle: when the pawns are touching you should take the pawn that is being touched. If you do not then you will be taken.

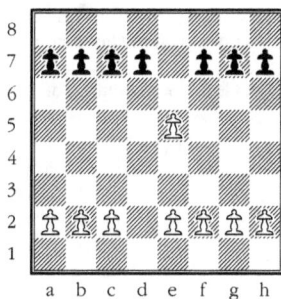

The position above is the result of the pawns touching and the White pawn taking the Black pawn it touched on e5, written **2.d4xe5** or **2.dxe5** or **2.de** .

4

2.3   Winning

. The object of the pawn game is to get one of your pawns **to the other side of the board and promote it to a queen**. In chess the pawn has a value of one point. It is the weakest man on the chess board, however if it reaches the other side of the board something special can happen. The pawn can become any piece (except another king). This is explained fully in Section 8.2. This is how you win in the pawn game. Now you must play through a few pawn games to get a feel for the movement of the pawns and to begin to understand strategy and to begin to think like a chess player.

Remember the rule is: when the pawns are touching you should take.

The only time you should not take is when you can win instead. For example:

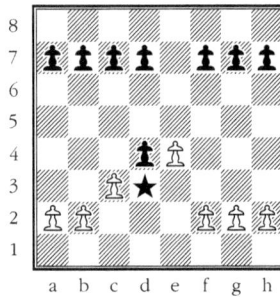

In the diagram above White has just moved his/her c-file pawn forward one square to c3. Black could take this pawn but if he/she did the White pawn on b2 would be touching and take the Black pawn back. However, if Black moves his d-file pawn one square forward to d3, then Black will win in two more moves! No White pawn can stop a Black pawn on d3.

Play a few games and learn the movement of the pawns.

3   The Knight

The next men we will add to the board are the knights. The knight has a very different movement from the pawns. The value of a knight is 3 and it moves in the shape of an upper-case L. This "L" movement can be in any direction. Here is a knight's "L" starting on square g1.

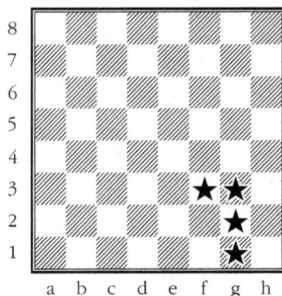

The best way to remember the movement of the knight is to count 0-1-2-3 as you move. Counting as the knight moves will help you learn the knight's movement without making a lot of mistakes. The knights start the game on b1 and b8 and g1 and g8.

The knight can also jump over other men. After both sides make two moves **1.e4 e5 2.Nf3 Nc6** this is a typical position for the knight-and-pawn game.

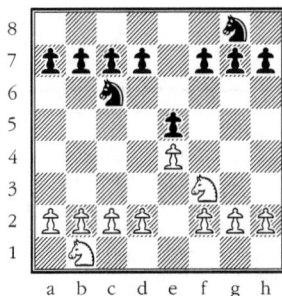

White can now move his knight from f3 to the opponent's side of the board with **3.Ng5**.

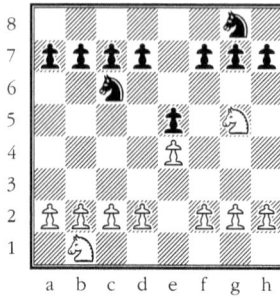

The key is to remember you do not move when you say zero. When you count the squares, the knight is standing on is 0 and as it moves you count 1-2-3. Notice that the knight standing on a dark square will end up on a light square after it moves, and a knight moving from a light square after moving will end up on a dark square.

In the diagram below if it was White's move he/she could take one of two different pawns by making a "L" as you count **0-1-2-3** and capturing the pawn or the knight can take the Black knight. Can you find the two pawns the knight can take? If the knight gets to the other side of the board you do not win. Only a pawn can win the pawn game by promoting to a queen. The knight can move backwards or to the side.

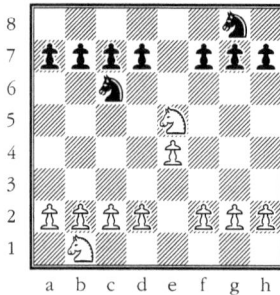

Here the White knight has just captured the Black pawn, written **3.Nxe5**. Notice the knight landed on the same square as the man it took. This is the only way a knight can capture a man. Now one of the Black knights can recapture the White knight in the middle of the board. Can you see how? Now play a few games with the knights-and-pawns in their starting positions, remembering to always start with **1.e4 e5** every time, then you're on your own to try to win. If you do not have a chess board with numbers and letters on the sides then just count with your left hand to the fifth pawn from the left side of the board and move it up two squares; this is the square e4. Now play some games using pawns and knights. Get familiar with the movement of the knights and the pawns working together to win.

4 The Bishop

Place the bishops on the chess board.

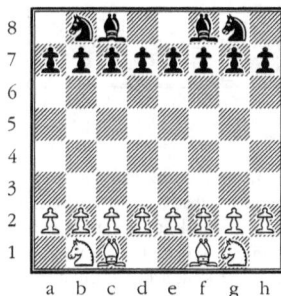

The bishop stands next to the knight. Like the knights there are two bishops. One bishop stands on a light square and the other on a dark square as shown above. When the pawns are present the bishop cannot move until the path is cleared of pawns. If the pawns are not present then the bishop is free to move on diagonals of the color it stands on.

After the example moves **1.e4 b5** we have this. White's bishop can move to any one of the squares marked with a star, plus one more!

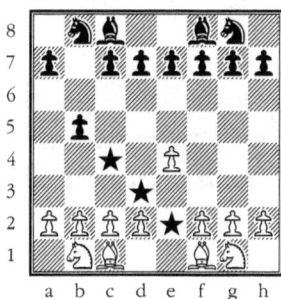

The Bishop can move one square or many squares at one time and it captures by taking the enemy man in its path and stopping there. So after **2.Bxb5** we have this position.

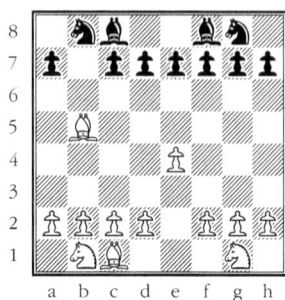

Unlike pawns, the bishops can move backwards as well as forward. Similar to the Knight's abilities in that respect and that is one of the reasons they both have the value of three points. Notice that White's dark squared bishop can move out to the square h6 and Black's light squared bishop can move to h3 taking the knight. Unlike the knight it cannot jump over men only the knight can do that in chess. Once again Bishops cannot win the pawn game if the bishop gets to the far end of the board. Then it can just start to move back however it must stay on the color squares it started out on. Now play a few games with the pawns, Knights and bishops and get a feel for how the bishops can help remove pawns, knights or enemy bishops clearing your path to victory.

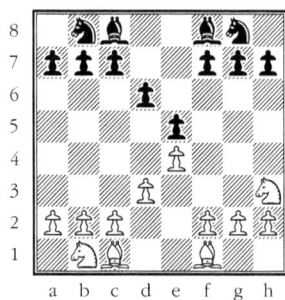

In the above position, can Black capture a knight?

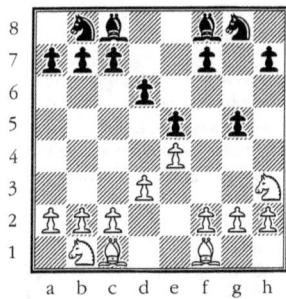

In the above position, how many different White men can capture a Black pawn?

5   The Rook

The next piece to add to the pawn game is the rook (or castle). They stand on the corner squares of the chess board and move in straight lines vertical or horizontal. They can also move backwards. In the diagram below the rooks are placed in their starting positions. They cannot move because the pawns and knights occupy the squares in front and next to them, and rooks cannot jump.

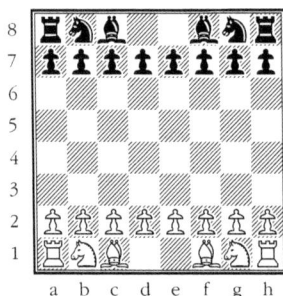

Rooks are valued at 5 points; they are now the strongest pieces on the chess board. They cannot move with the pawn and knight blocking them. So, to move your rook you have to move the pawn forward or move the knight away, as both players have done in this diagram. Note that the White rook can move from where it stands a3 to h3 in one move. The rook that is not blocked by anything can move as far as you wish.

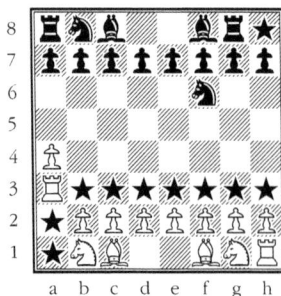

The rooks also cannot win the pawn game if they reach the other side of the board. Play a few games using the rooks, Knights, bishops and pawns to get a feel for the rook's movement and how this very strong piece can help you win. The diagrams below demonstrate White's rook taking on e7, written **4.Rxe7**

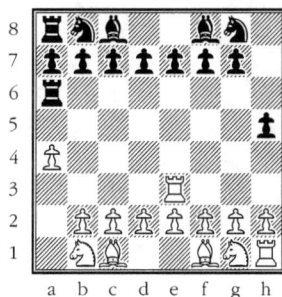

and then Black's rook responding by taking the pawn on a4, written **4...Rxa4**.

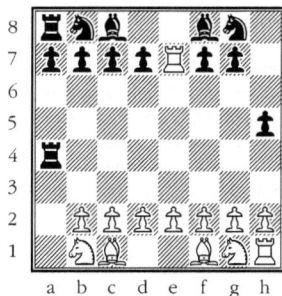

A few pointers: first any man can take any other man. A pawn can take a rook but only if it is touching the rook. When the pawns are touching you should take and that includes any man they are touching not just the pawns. When you can take a man of the same or higher value you should.

In the diagram below Black has just moved his rook over to h4. What should White do?

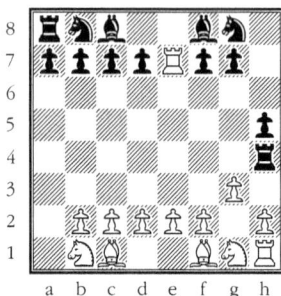

The answer should be easy using the principle I have given you "when the pawns touch take" the man it is touching. White should play gxh4 capturing the rook. By removing the enemy men your way will become clear and you have chances to win. Whenever your opponent moves a man you should first ask yourself can I take it? By looking at every man you have you can assess whether you can capture the man or not. This is part of the discipline needed to be good at chess. Chess is a thinking game but at this stage it is a seeing and knowing game. What I mean is you must first know that you can take a man by seeing it can be taken. Then you must know that you should in fact capture the man that is threatened to be taken. If you cannot take the man your next question is what is the man trying to do? Perhaps it is threatening to take one of your men that are not protected. Yes, thought is applied to this but it's more procedure than deep thinking at this point just looking and seeing. You are just learning and because there is much more to learn I am keeping it simple. So, ask the magic questions every time your opponent moves. Can you take the man he/she moved? If not where can that man move to, what is it trying to do? Look hard to be sure and take your time so you get the answer right. This is important for your rapid development.

6 The Royalty

The Queen and King enter the game together.

Now that you are familiar with the movement of the four men we have introduced so far, it's time to bring the King and the Queen to the chess board.

The king is the most important piece, and his fighting value is 4 points when enough other pieces are removed from the board so that he can roam without much fear of being attacked. He can move in any direction but can only move one square at a time, as shown by the stars in the diagram below. The king must be protected at all times.

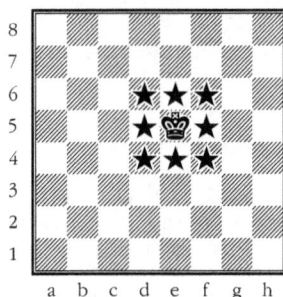

The Queen is the strongest piece on the chess board; she has a value of 9 points. For this reason, you should not lose her or give her away for a lesser man. She moves like a bishop and a rook put together, similar to the king however she can move many squares in one move as long as she is not blocked by any men. In the center of an open board she can choose between 27 squares!

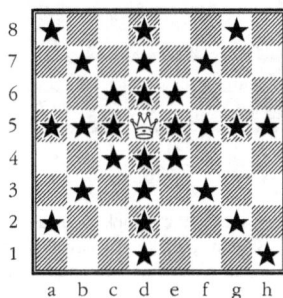

In the starting position, the pair stands in the middle of the chess board with a White Queen standing on a light square and a Black Queen standing on a dark square, with the Kings on the remaining empty squares, as shown below.

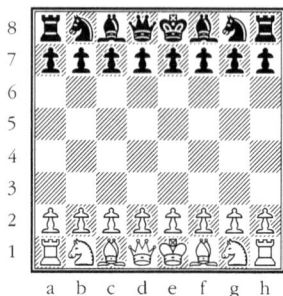

6.1   Take the King!

Now that we have introduced the kings, winning is now done by winning the king. No longer is getting a pawn to the other side of the board winning. We will start with "take the king" rules: if you capture the opponent's king you win.

In the diagram below after **1.e4 e5** the White queen moved like a bishop to the square h5 and Black replied by moving the knight to a position to take the queen **2.Qh5 Nf6**.

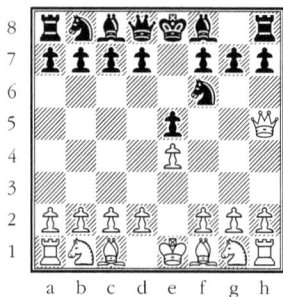

Now the queen can move like a rook sideways and take the pawn in the middle of the board **3.Qxe5**. Should she take this pawn? Yes. She would then be in a position to take the king. As Black what would you do to prevent this? You have two possibilities. Can you find them?

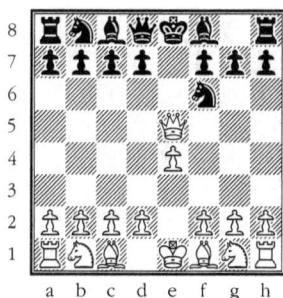

The first possibility is you can move your bishop in front of your king interposing. Another option is move your queen out blocking. If you do anything else White will capture your king and the game will be lost.

Now should the White queen take the Black queen?

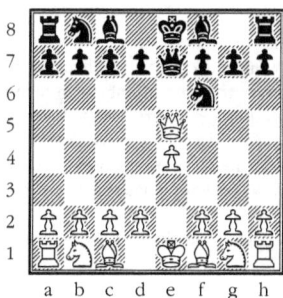

The answer is yes. Every time you can take a man of the same value for now (while you're a beginner) you should. It's that simple. Now play a few games playing take the king.

Remember, it's time for discipline in your way of playing and thinking. Every time your opponent moves ask yourself: can I take it? If you can the next thing is: should I take it? If you should not take it <u>one more question</u> must be asked. That question is: what is the man trying to do? Can it take one of your men? Where can it go? You must see clearly exactly what it can do from where it is standing.

In this position the White bishop moved out and attacked the Black king. The Black player did not ask the questions. All she saw was: I can attack White's king. So, she moved her bishop out to attack the White king.

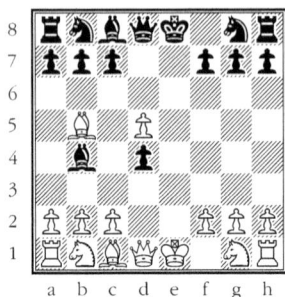

Now what should White do? Take the king and win. Now play many games with all the pieces until you can move them without making mistakes. Take the king and win!

6.2   Check and Checkmate

After a student has learned to take the king and has gotten well acquainted with this game we must now introduce the word Check to the game. Check is said as a warning to the opposing player that you are about to take his/her king. This is said immediately after making the move that threatens to take the king. We have not done this until now and as a rule now as we move forward you can no longer take the king. You must now also say check when you are threatening the king with any man.

There are three ways of getting out of check, which should be considered in this order:

1) Take the man that has your king checked. In the diagram above, White's queen has just checked the Black king, however Black can get out of check. What is the best move?

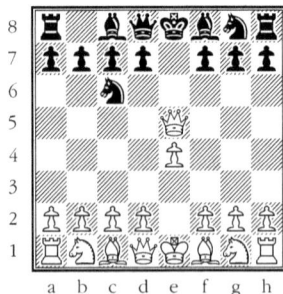

The best move would be to take the man that is checking the king. The Black knight takes the White queen **3...Nxe5**.

2) Block the man that is checking the king (diagram below).

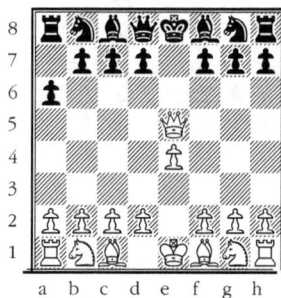

The White queen has just moved into position to check Black's king. Black can **interpose** this check three different ways. He can move the bishop in front of the king.

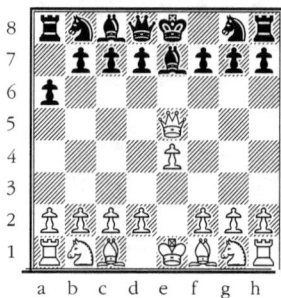

Black can also move the knight or the queen in front of his king, as shown below. He must make one of these moves to get out of check.

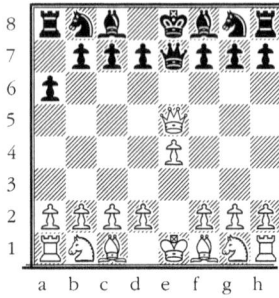

3) Run with the king out of the way so he will not be in check. Run away! (Diagram below) In this position Black could have interposed with his queen or knight but chose to move his king over to get out of check with **3…Kf8**.

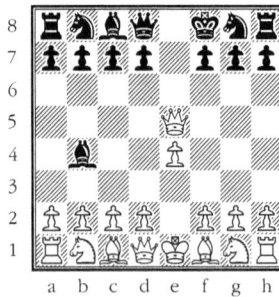

When a player's king is in check, if he cannot get out of check he is in **checkmate**. In the diagram below, the Black king is in check by the White queen. Every move the king can make here is still check, and his entire army cannot help, therefore the Black king is **checkmated**. Checkmate is the object of the game.

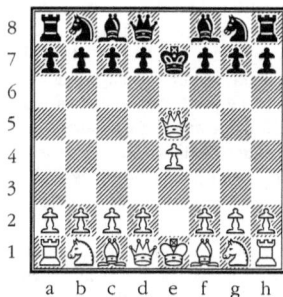

Now we are beginning to play real chess. So, we are no longer playing take the king we are playing to checkmate the king. One must say check to his/her opponent when they have the king in check and the second player must get out of check. If they cannot this is called checkmate and the game is over. One will realize that this is not so easy to do. It is much more difficult than just taking the king. All you have been taught before this has been to get to this point. It was just my fun new way to get you here. Continue playing some games with the new rule of saying check to warn your opponent and check mate to win. After the student has played and gotten used to this new rule the real fun begins. Now we can start to learn the patterns that I need you to memorize. This is called pattern recognition. In chess you must learn to recognize patterns. Next is the first pattern I want you to learn.

7 The Matrix Attack

The Matrix attack is the first pattern that I teach my students. This is much better as a beginner opening than the Scholar's Mate (1.e4 e5 2.Bc4 Bc5 3.Qh5 Nc6 4.Qxf7#) or all other openings I have seen. Reason number one is the Scholar's Mate can be stopped by the move 2...Nf6. For this reason alone, I have never thought the Scholar's Mate was that scholarly but nevertheless instructive. Perhaps that's why it's called the scholar's mate. The number two reason is there are several instructive mistakes beginners make as they learn the Matrix attack. The Matrix attack is perfect for allowing the beginner to make certain mistakes that allow for corrections that will become the base of understanding producing fast chess understanding. The moves of the Matrix attack are very instructive and begin a pattern of attack I have realized is the key to quicken the pace of understanding for every chess player/chess teacher. The student is taught move order, focal points of attack and defense along with pattern recognition.

The first moves we have made in every game so far has been **1.e4 e5**: White moves his pawn to the square e4 and Black moves his pawn to e5. This pawn situation is called meeting and you should have made that connection. Now White moves his queen to h5, **2.Qh5**. This is the Matrix attack.

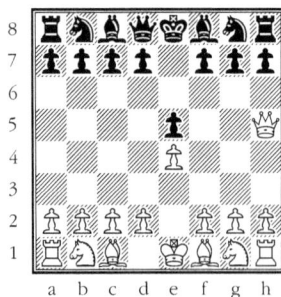

Pattern 1

What should Black do? There are several mistakes Black can make here and you need to recognize each mistake and what you should do when you see one of these errors. The first mistake is if Black plays the move **2...g6?** attacking White's queen.

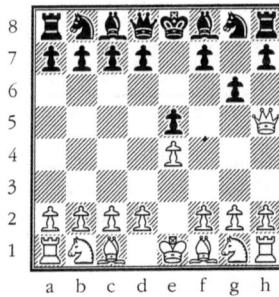

White should then play **3.Qxe5+**. This is a **fork**: one man (the queen) attacks two enemy men.

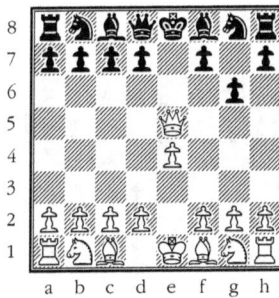

However Black interposes what will White play? **4. Qxh8** winning the rook. End of pattern 1.

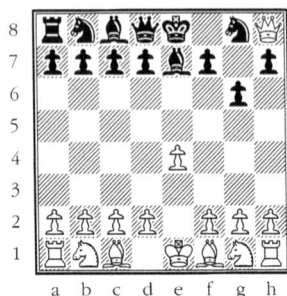

This fork pattern must be played repeatedly until you have memorized this short pattern. The move **2...g6?** is a huge mistake and White must capitalize on Black's error. In the position above the moves were **1.e4 e5 2.Qh5 g6 3.Qxe5 Be7 4.Qxh8**. White is now ahead by 5 points. This pattern must be remembered. Take your time and get it memorized. This pattern and others will be the patterns that will make you an advanced player quickly by the end of this book.

Pattern 2
The next pattern is similar and connects to the first. As you play along try to see the connection.
This position started with the moves. **1.e4 e5 2.Qh5** here Black plays **2...Nf6** this move is another mistake by Black as you can see the player with the Black men is not asking the questions after White moves.

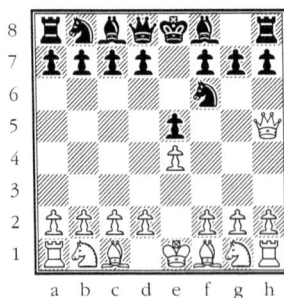

Can you see the reason why Black's last move is a mistake? The move is bad because now the White queen can win a pawn for free. The pawn on e5 is "hanging." Hanging is the chess term that means the man is not protected and can be taken for free. Now you should memorize this sequence of moves. You have to remember what to do when Black makes these mistakes.

Pattern 3

Again the moves start out the same 1.**e4 e5 2. Qh5** Nc6 here Black plays the correct move protecting his pawn. **3. Bc4 Nf6?** What should White do?

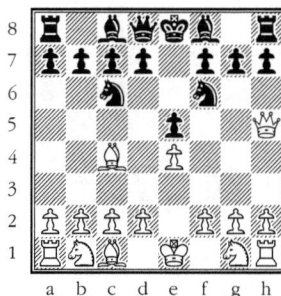

4.Qxf7# the Matrix version of the Scholar's Mate checkmate! These are the three basic mistakes Black will make. Now you know what to do when these mistakes are made. You have just learned the main idea of the Matrix attack and now play these patterns over and over until you have memorized them.

This is one position you are aiming for in the Matrix attack.

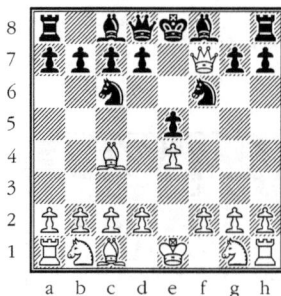

This is what you are trying to do with this plan: checkmating your opponent in 4 moves. This is an easy plan to remember. The best way to remember this is not only to remember the moves but to also remember the plan.

Pattern 4
1.e4 e5 2.Qh5 Nc6 3.Bc4 g6 here Black makes the right moves to hold his e5 pawn
and stop the checkmate by White.

Now look at the position above. If you are playing the way I have instructed
you, you will ask yourself now: can I take the pawn Black just moved? The answer is
yes. <u>Should</u> you take it is the next question, and the answer is no. The reason being a
pawn would then take your queen. Since you cannot take it the next question is what is
that man trying to do? It's trying to stop a checkmate and threatening to take your queen.
Using this system of asking and answering questions you will play without making
unnecessary mistakes. So now since you must move your queen where should you
move her? You would look at every possibility the queen has and choose her best move.
In the above position what would that move be? The move that is best is **4.Qf3** (diagram
below) this move repositions the queen getting her out of harm's way and now she is
once again threatening checkmate on f7.

Now, just so we can practice this pattern, let's say Black plays the bad move **4...Nd4?** ignoring the threat and attacking the White queen. What is White's best move? White's best move is **5.Qxf7#** checkmate.

Practice this plan until you have it memorized.

How does Black stop White from checkmating him with this plan? One answer is Black to play the move **4...Nf6** blocking checkmate.

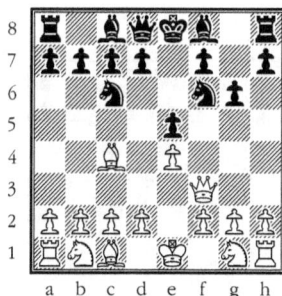

In this position White attacks the focal point f7 one last time with the move **5.Qb3** forming a union called a **battery** with the bishop aiming at f7, and Black responds this time with the move **5...Qe7** protecting the focal point the f7 square.

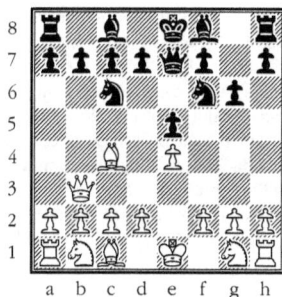

This is the beginners Matrix attack. This is the first pattern I recognized as a chess player. You must now memorize this pattern and when you have you are ready to begin to learn the game on a higher level. I suggest that you play many games after you reach this position to get familiar with the game of chess. You will have to find another way to checkmate Black or get checkmated by Black and this is all part of the learning process. Now you should finish developing your men and castle your king. The Matrix attack will not always result in checkmate. So that is how you continue the game. Perfect practice makes you perfect. It's simple the more you practice the chess way of thinking and the patterns I have shown you the better you will get. Losing and making mistakes is part of chess. Don't get discouraged if you make mistakes just correct your errors in the next game. If other moves are played by your opponent just use the questions and play and see what happens, learning as you go. For example, after **1.e4 e5 2.Nf3 f6?**

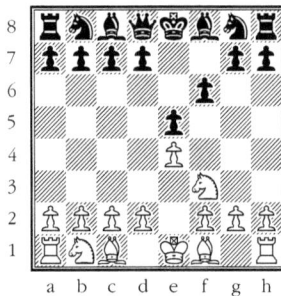

White can now play **3.Nxe5 fxe5 4.Qh5+ g6 5.Qxe5+ forking** and, no matter how Black interposes, White's queen will take the rook on h8. The **matrix** pattern unleashed again!

The next step in my method of learning and teaching chess is to teach the Two Knights Defense. As you will see the focal point is the same square f7. The big difference is White uses different attackers. In chess it is not strong that you bring your Queen out early unless you have a very good reason. I taught this in the Matrix chapter to teach several specific things. Mainly that the f7 square is the focus of your attack, and the power and versatility of the queen can be overwhelming. The other lessons were basic chess logic, direct attack of the king, the common mistakes to look out for, and then how Black can stop these premature attacks. This is the best way to get a new player to understand what is really going on in a game of chess. This method has worked well for me and my students. You should play both White and Black side of these openings to improve fast.

8   The Last Three Rules

There are three special rules that have not yet been important to the fundamental concepts of piece movements and the focal points at f2/f7. They are: castling, pawn promotion, and pawn *en passant* (in passing) capture.

8.1   Castling

When the king and rook are in positions below and neither piece has moved, **castling** is allowed. Castling is the only move in chess where you can move two men in only one move.

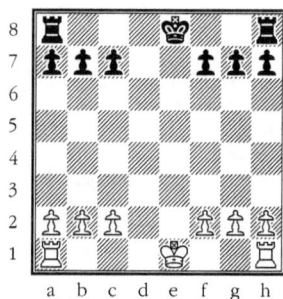

Here White castles on his kingside, or "castles short," which is written **O-O**. The king moves over two squares, toward the rook on his right, and the rook moves to the square the king crossed, all in one move, resulting in the position below.

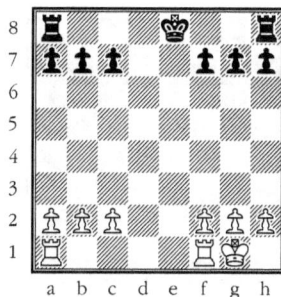

Then Black castles on his queenside, or "castles long," which is written **...O-O-O**. The king <u>moves over two squares</u>, toward the rook on HIS right, and the rook moves to the square the king crossed, all in one move, resulting in the position below.

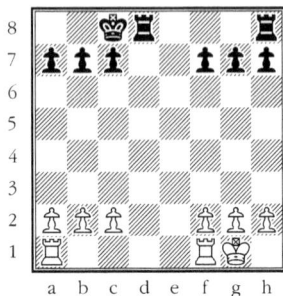

Castling is done in most games to protect the king and activate the rook.

The limitations on castling are:

1) the king must never have moved,
2) the rook must never have moved,
3) the king must not move out of, through, or into, check.

8.2   Promotion

The pawn is the man with the least value on the board. However, if it reaches the other side of the board it can become any piece except another king. This is known as **pawn promotion** and the lowly pawn is the only one that has this power. In the position below White's pawn has made it to his 7th rank. One more move and it can promote.

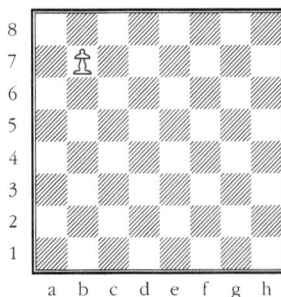

In the diagram below the pawn has moved to the 8th rank and become a queen. This is how you promote a pawn. What you choose to replace the pawn is up to you as a player. Would you have chosen to promote your pawn to a queen?

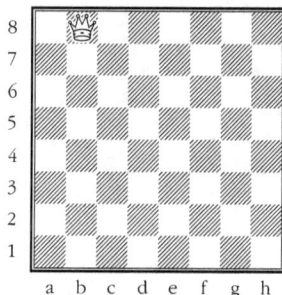

8.3   *En Passant*

There is one rule I have left out on purpose until now. This is the *en passant* or "in passing" pawn capture rule. It is a rule that most of my players take quite a while to understand, be aware of, and use properly. When one of your pawns has moved to the enemy's side of the board he gets a super power. In the position below after the moves **1.c4 f5 2. c5 f4** both players have moved their pawns past the centerline onto the enemy side of the board, on c5 and f4.

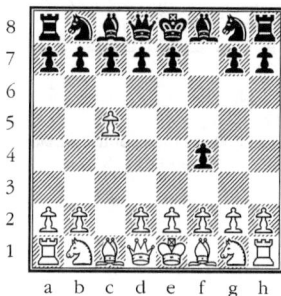

Now it is Whites move, who plays the move **3.e4**. This move passes the Black f4-pawn without stopping on e3 giving the Black pawn a normal chance to capture it.

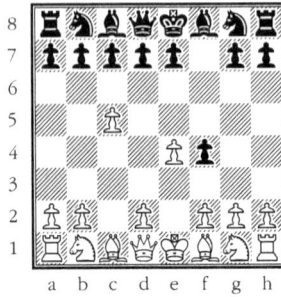

This is where the special power kicks in and the Black pawn can now take the White pawn *en passant*, which is French for "in passing," **as if it had stopped** on e3, which is written **3...f4xe3** or **3...fxe3**. or **3...fe** .

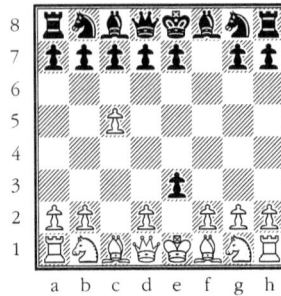

This is the only capture in chess where the capturing man does not land on the square occupied by the captured man. It can only be executed on the very next move after the opposing pawn passed it by.

9 The Two Knights Defense

9.1 Introduction to Real Chess

I cannot state too much that these have been patterns for beginners to rapidly learn and have fun with the game, not the best possible moves to play in a chess game. This way of learning has given me the pleasure of teaching many good players and they all started from here. This works better than any other method I have ever seen in all my years teaching and playing chess. These positions can actually occur in a game of players of a certain level and hopefully it is you who are the one putting the player in checkmate. All you have to do is remember what you are supposed to do and if you forget a move follow my principles for analyzing the position. This should bring the correct continuation to your mind. As usual once we reach a certain point it's time to move on and learn more. In chess there is always more to learn and that's what makes chess such a wonderful experience. Henceforth when I use the term develop your pieces what I mean is continue to move the men off the back rank forward into the game. Remember you should practice these moves and try to play many games with this as a guide, getting familiar with what might and can happen. At this point you should not be playing the Matrix anymore. The Matrix occurred to me watching my older brother play with his friends for a year 1972 to 1973. One day I asked if I could play. The room was surprised because no one thought I knew how to play. I had only sat quietly observing from my seat. I beat all of them using the Matrix. For me it is just an opening system for learning. There is one player I know who uses the Matrix regularly and has for years and he is an expert chess player. His name is Parham, every chess player has his/her own style and that is his. If you wish you can become a Parham/Matrix player but I don't recommend it.

9.2 Your First Opening

As mentioned in the last chapter this opening is once again focused on the square f7. Black is the side that is deploying the Two Knights Defense. The first moves move are **1.e4 e5 2.Nf3** this move attacks the pawn on e5 so Black protects it by developing his knight **2...Nc6** then **3.Bc4** attacking f7. **3... Nf6** this is the Two Knights defense. It is easy to remember because, as you see, the Black player meets White's plan by bringing both his knights into play first.

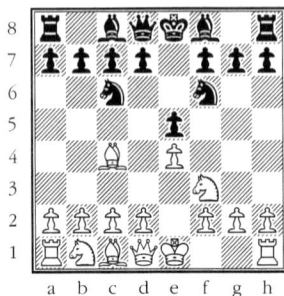

Now it is White's move and here White plays **4.Ng5** attacking the f7 square with two pieces. The knight and the bishop are now both hitting the focal point f7. Only the Black king defends f7.

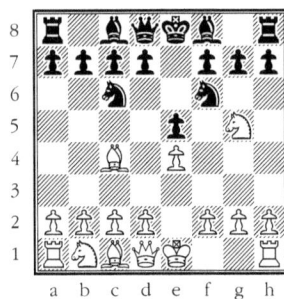

9.3   The Threats

There is only one good way to stop the knight or the bishop from taking on f7. Before we see the one move that should be played we will examine bad moves beginners make and what you should do when these moves are made against you. The first incorrect move is **4...Qe7?** This move looks good arithmetically (2 defenders versus 2 attackers) but it does not actually stop White from taking the pawn on f7 with **5.Bxf7+** .

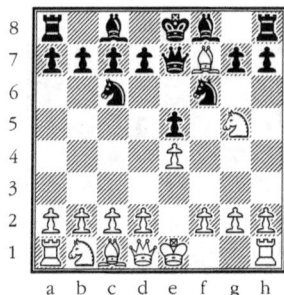

If the Queen takes here she will be captured by the knight and Black will be losing because she is worth 9 points. This is very bad for Black, and now he must move his king to **5...Kd8**. A good try for White here is to move **6.Bb3** and if **6...h6** trying to chase the knight away, the knight jumps in with a **7.Nxf7+** fork and then **8.Nxh8** winning the Rook.

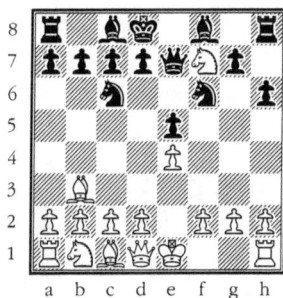

The king must move and the knight will take the rook on h8 and once again Black is behind in points and losing. This is a short pattern that you should learn to use whenever Black plays this way against you. After you reach these positions you must play the game out and try to win. The easiest way for White to win is to finish developing and then start exchanging. This is how you practice to get better.

The next bad move we will look at after the Two Knights moves **1.e4 e5 2. Nf3 Nc6 3.Bc4 Nf6 4.Ng5** is **4...h6?** This bad move just forces the knight to jump in with **5.Nxf7** and, as you can see, another knight **fork** of the rook on h8 and the queen on e8. (Since the queen is the piece that has a higher value she should move and allow the rook to be taken, but Black is losing.)

34

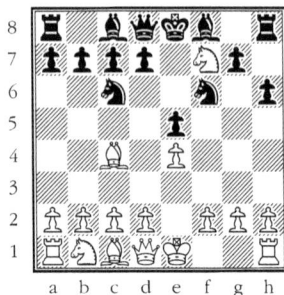

All this amounts to the move **4...h6?** not being good for Black. Again, I want you to play the rest of the game to see what happens and who wins. You must play and see to get better and that means every position should be played out to get better.

9.4   Good Defense

Now we will look at what Black should play when they are attacked this way. Going back to the Two Knights position **1.e4 e5 2.Nf3 Nc6 3.Bc4 Nf6 4.Ng5**

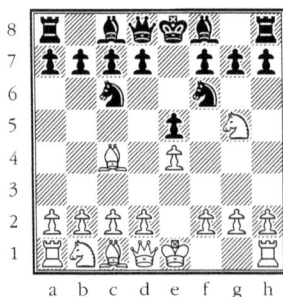

the only correct defense is **4...d5** blocking the bishop from ganging up on the focal point f7.

Now as I have stated earlier when the pawns touch you should take as a beginner and here that is the right move: **5.exd5 Nxd5** and White can now try **6.Nxf7**. This **piece sacrifice** is known as the "Fried Liver" attack.

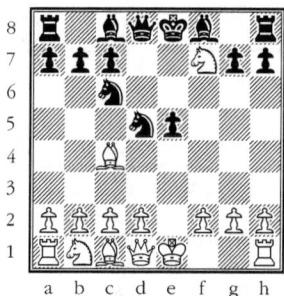

Since the knight on f7 forks queen and rook, Black's king must march forward with **6... Kxf7 7.Qf3+ Qf6 8.Bxd5+ Be6 9.Bxe6 Kxe6 10.Qb3+ Kd7 11.Qxb7**

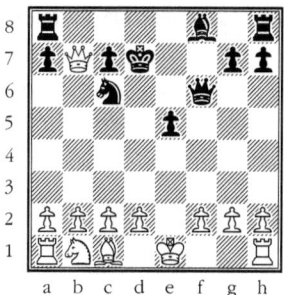

This pattern is very important. All the moves and reactions are part of the principles I have been teaching you. This move sequence must be repeated and memorized. In the position above, it is Black's move and White is threatening to take the Rook on a8. What should Black do here? The move I recommend is **11...Bc5**, counter-attacking on the f2 square focal point!

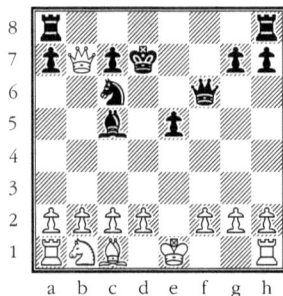

This is the focal point that only the White king protects and now the queen and the bishop attack it together. This move also connects the Black rooks so they now protect each other. So, what should White do to protect the square f2 that is being attacked? The best move is **12.O-O** and in interesting continuation then is **12...Raf8 13.Nc3 Bxf2+ 14.Kh1 Qh4 15.h3 Rf3 16.Kh2 Rxh3+ 17.gxh3 Qg3+ 18.Kh1 Qxh3#** checkmate. As you have just seen, in certain positions you can force your opponent to make moves to help you win the game. This pattern is one that must be remembered and it is eighteen moves. This is what chess players call a **stem game** for their understanding. You might be thinking that you cannot remember all eighteen moves, but you can and must. I know it seems hard but you can do it. Once you do you will realize just how much you are capable of on the chess board. How do you remember all this? You will have to play these moves over and over until you do. The best way is to understand the plan along with the moves and it should make the process much easier.

The next learning step requires you to leave this all behind and take another approach to your opening strategy. This new approach is called the Italian Game.

10 The Italian Game

The thing I love about my approach to teaching chess is how the ideas connect, giving the student a firm foundation. Notice how the openings all are similar, aiming at the f7/f2 square. And Black/White must try to fend off the initial attack.

The first moves here **1.e4 e5 2.Nf3 Nc6 3.Bc4** are the same as the Two Knights Defense. The different move is made by Black on move three **3...Bc5**. This is the Italian Game, also called the *Giuoco Piano*, Italian for "quiet game."

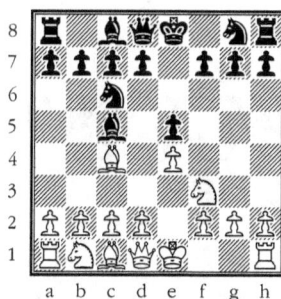

4.O-O White castles early to protect his king and get him out of the center of the board.
4... Nf6 Black places his knight on the correct developing square, attacking White's center and preparing to castle.
5.d3 protecting his pawn, freeing his bishop and trying to pin the knight with his bishop (Bg5) if he gets the chance. About pinning: a pin is when a defending man cannot move without exposing a man of higher value to attack. Pinning a man means the man pinned cannot move without a very good reason.
5... h6 Black sees what White wants to do and prevents the pin.

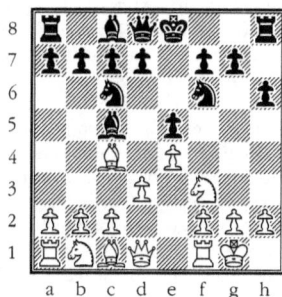

6.Be3 White develops his bishop.

6… Bxe3 Black asked the question "should I take that?" and answered with yes because if he does not he would be taken.

7.fxe3 White asked the question should he take the piece and the obvious answer is yes because Black has just taken White's bishop and to keep the score even he must.

7… d6 Black plans to develop his bishop to the g4 square where he will have the White knight on f3 pinned.

8.h3 White prevents Black from pinning his knight.

8…Bd7 9.Qe2 developing the queen and connecting the rooks.

9…O-O Black castles, developing without moving the same piece twice, a basic opening principle.

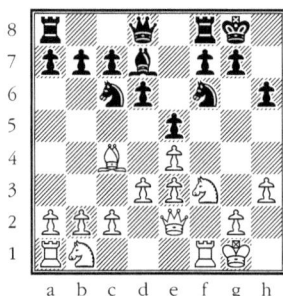

10. Nc3 White develops his knight to the center of the board, not to a3, because unless you have a good reason, "Knights on the rim are grim" a chess adage that helps remember that a knight has less options when you place them on the edge of the board. Here you will note that if you put the knight on a3 it would only have 2 possible moves to go back where it just moved from or the b5 square. When you put it on c3 where it belongs, it has the squares b1, a4, d5, b5 and d1. The knight having all these options makes it much stronger than when you develop it to the edge of the chess board.

10…Qe7   The rooks can now move to the center of the board on the back row or eight rank. To develop in most cases, you are moving a piece off the back row and placing on the best square you can find.

11.Rad1 the rook develops from the corner to the center where it can be a help breaking up the center if needed. Note that the rooks move to where he has a possibility of being effective. The rook moving to let's say e1 would have been less effective because the squares in front of it are blocked and will be for a while. The square d1 is much more promising if White gets a chance to play e4 at some point then the rook will be exerting its influence on that square also. White's development is complete at this time.

11…Rad8 Black does the same thing for the same reasons as White.

8
7
6
5
4
3
2
1

a b c d e f g h

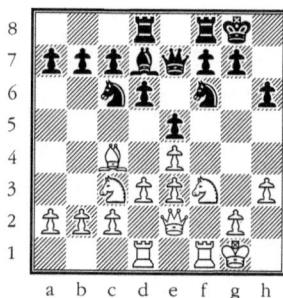

Note that Black could have moved this rook to e8, but that move would take all the mobility from the other rook on f8. In a chess game you want your pieces to have as much mobility as possible at all times.

You have now reached the position you will practice for this variation and once again you must learn it and practice it. I suggest that you open a chesskid.com account if you are a child or another site if your older. Some of you have friends and family to play against others have a community that will allow you to go out and try this at a chess club or barber shop or maybe even chess in the park. Others will only have internet opponents or themselves to play but either way you need to practice a lot to get good. This is an excellent way to start your chess life and I hope you agree. If you have followed my instructions in this book you should be competitive with players of your strength and even surprise well-seasoned players with your skills. I wish you the best chess ever and thank you for allowing me to be your chess teacher. Love life and chess!!!